# U.S. Army Fighting Vehicles

RICHARD BARTLETT

Heinemann Library
Chicago, Illinois

Designed by Herman Adler Design
Photo research by Bill Broyles
Printed and bound in the United States by Lake Book
Manufacturing, Inc.

08 07 06 05 04
10 9 8 7 6 5 4 3 2 1

**Library of Congress Cataloging-in-Publication Data**
Bartlett, Richard.
  U.S. Army fighting vehicles / by Richard Bartlett.
      p. cm. -- (U.S. Armed Forces)
Summary: Provides an overview of the types of vehicles used
by the United States Army and their purposes.
Includes bibliographical references and index.
    ISBN 1-4034-0189-6 (HC), 1-4034-0446-1 (Pbk.)
    1. Vehicles, Military--United States--Juvenile literature. [1.
Vehicles, Military.  2. Armored vehicles, Military.  3. United
States. Army--Weapons systems.]  I. Title.  II. U.S. Armed
Forces (Series)
UG618.B363 2003
623.7'4'0973--dc21

                    2002015404

**Acknowledgments**
The author and publishers are grateful to the following for
permission to reproduce copyright material:
Cover photograph by Charles O'Rear/Corbis
Title page, pp. 5B, 7, 8, 9, 10, 11, 12, 14, 16, 19, 20, 21, 22,
28, 29, 30, 31, 32 Department of Defense; p. 4 AFP/Corbis;
p. 5T Library of Congess; p. 13 Katsumi Kasahara/AP Wide
World Photo; pp. 15, 17B Bettmann/Corbis; p. 17T Froilan
Gallardo/AP Wide World Photo; p. 24 Robin Adshead/The
Military Picture Library/Corbis; p. 25 Stephen Morton/Getty
Images; pp. 26, 27, 41 Lockheed Martin; p. 33 Systems &
Electronics Inc; pp. 34, 35 General Dynamics; p. 36 Richard
Zellner/Sikorsky Aircraft/AP Wide World Photo; p. 38 Bryan
Mitchell/Getty Images; p. 39 Reuters NewMedia Inc./Corbis;
pp. 40, 44, 45 Northrop Grumman Corporation; p. 42 U.S.
Army; p. 43 AAI Corporation; icon (flag) Corbis

Special thanks to Lt. Col. G.A. Lofaro for his help in the
preparation of this book.
Every effort has been made to contact copyright holders of
any material reproduced in this book. Any omissions will be
rectified in subsequent printings if notice is given to
publisher.

**Note to the Reader:** Some words are shown in
bold, **like this.** You can find out what they mean
by looking in the glossary.

# Contents

# U.S. Army Fighting Vehicles: Modern-Day Chariots of Fire

Since early times, vehicles have been used to fight wars. Roman gladiators had their chariots (carriages pulled by horses), some with up to six **horsepower.** Today, the United States. Army has a battle tank with 1,500 horsepower. Throughout history, one fact has always been true. Whether it ran on hay or fuel, the faster and more powerful an army's fighting vehicles were, the better chance it had of winning in battle.

Since it was formed more than 200 years ago, the U.S. Army has understood how important fighting vehicles are. It has always worked to have horses, tanks, and aircraft that were better than the enemy's. By using the latest technology, the U.S. Army has developed a group of combat vehicles that is the most powerful in all the world.

The technology of tanks has been used to design other vehicles. These missile launchers have tracks, not wheels. They can move over rough ground, day or night.

In 1865, Union soldiers removed this artillery from a Confederate fort they had captured.

These World War I soldiers were glad to have their modern equipment.

# On the move long ago

People who have studied the Civil War (1861–1865) think that soldiers used about 100,000 horses for riding. As many as 1.5 million draft animals (horses, mules, and donkeys) were also used. The draft animals pulled the artillery and wagons.

The first caterpillar track (the "wheels" of the tank) was invented in 1770 in England. During a war in Europe in the 1850s, the track was put on farmers' tractors so they could move through mud and transport equipment.

Tanks were not used until the end of World War I (1914–1918). The British first used combat tanks in 1916 and the French used them one year later. The U.S. Tank Corps then began to develop its own tanks. In World War I, the U.S. Army used a tank based on the French model.

# M1 Abrams: King of the Battlefield

Since the beginning of the 1900s, the **armored** tank has been important in land battles. During this period, the U.S. Army's M1 Abrams Main Battle Tank has been one of the best fighting vehicles in the world. It has enough high-speed firepower to destroy any enemy armored fighting vehicle. It can be used in any type of weather, day or night, and under all combat conditions.

Since the first Abrams battle tank was produced in the early 1980's, over 8,000 more tanks have been built. In the last twenty years four different versions have been made. They are the original M1, and three improved models, the M1A1, M1A2, and the M1A2SEP (System Enhancement Package). Here are some features of the three improved versions.

- Weight: nearly 70 tons. This is equal to the weight of 27 full-sized trucks.

- Top Speed: about 40 miles (64 kilometers) per hour

- Engine: 1500 **horsepower** gas turbine engine

- Crew: four, including the commander, the gunner, the loader, and the driver

- Guns: 120mm armor-piercing main gun and three machine guns. It also can fire special smoke grenades, that hide the Abrams M1A2 from its enemies.

## Know It

Part of a gun's name refers to the size of its ammunition. 120mm means the ammunition is 120 millimeters (4.8 inches) in diameter (across). The diameter is called the caliber. If the caliber is shown as a decimal, the measurement is in inches. Two of the larger caliber guns that police officers carry are the .38 and the .45, both of which are tiny compared to the M1A2.

- **Forward-Looking InfraRed (FLIR):** This is a system that helps the gunner to locate the enemy at night and in the heavy smoke that sometimes covers the battlefield. In the Gulf War (1991), for example, a similar system helped the Abrams find and destroy Iraqi tanks even when the crew was surrounded by the thick, black smoke from burning oil wells.

- Warfare protection: Each Abrams M1A1 and M1A2 has special equipment that can protect the crew from nuclear, biological, and chemical attacks.

During the Gulf War, about 1,900 M1A1 tanks were used in Saudi Arabia. Only 18 were taken out of service because of battle damage. Mechanics were able to fix 9 of those. No Abrams crewmembers died.

The all-powerful M1 Abrams Main Battle Tank is a commonly used weapon. The warfare protection equipment includes one system that provides clean air for the crew and another that can detect chemical agents.

# M2/M3 Bradley Fighting Vehicle

This Bradley Fighting Vehicle is being driven across a temporary bridge.

The Bradley Fighting Vehicles are smaller and lighter than the M1 Abrams Battle Tanks. The Bradley's three main roles are to transport soldiers (also called troops) to the battlefield, provide cover fire to soldiers already on the ground, and to destroy enemy tanks and other fighting vehicles. The Bradley carries a wide range of weapons.

The two main kinds of Bradley Fighting Vehicles are the M2 Infantry Fighting Vehicle and the M3 Cavalry Fighting Vehicle. The M2 can carry up to six ground troops, or **infantry**, directly to the battlefield.

The M3 operates as a scout vehicle. It carries a pair of scouts, more weapons, and additional **communications** equipment.

All Bradley Fighting Vehicles are amphibious, which means they can work on water and on land. To work on water, the crew inflates a **pontoon,** which keeps the 12-ton vehicle afloat. Then, by using its tracks (the cover on the wheels that goes around when the wheels move) for **propulsion**, the Bradley can move through the water at up to four miles (about six kilometers) per hour.

The Bradley Fighting Vehicle's main weapon is a gun that can fire armor-piercing or highly explosive ammunition. This weapon can hit a target even while the vehicle is moving at high speeds and over very rough ground. Another weapon is the TOW Antitank Missile. It can be fired at targets more than two miles (three kilometers) away. It can destroy any armored vehicle.

The TOW in Tow missile stands for **T**ube-launched, **O**ptically-tracked, and **W**ire-guided. The missile is shot from a tube. The gunner keeps the target in his sight. A pair of wires attached to the back of the missile guides it, based on where the gunner is aiming.

These ground troops salute from inside the Bradley M2 Infantry Fighting Vehicle.

# M88A2 Hercules Heavy Recovery Vehicle

When a 70-ton M1 Abrams Battle Tank breaks down, you cannot call a tow truck. Or can you? There is only one vehicle in the world that can lift and tow such heavyweights as the Abrams. It is the M88A2 Hercules Heavy Recovery Vehicle. This is not a fighting vehicle, but it is the only vehicle that can get a stuck Abrams tank moving again.

The Hercules is an armored vehicle like those that it rescues. However, the Hercules does not use weapons to perform its missions. Instead, it uses a boom and a winch. The boom is a long arm that can swing out in any direction. It can lift 35 tons. The main winch, a combination of wheels, pulleys, and cables, can pull up to 140,000 pounds (63,500 kilograms). The winch can also be used to tow vehicles that cannot

Hercules is strong enough to lift this tank back onto its treads.

Hercules tows a disabled tank through water.

operate under their own power. The Hercules Heavy Recovery Vehicle has a three-person crew. It can operate in all types of weather and on any kind of terrain (ground).

The Hercules was tested after it was built. In one test it had to tow a 70-ton Abrams tank up a steep, muddy, slippery hill. The Hercules passed the test by successfully towing the huge Abrams up a 25 percent grade. The larger the grade, the steeper the hill. Most mountain passes you might travel over in your family car are around 5 to 10 percent grade. Just think of the M88A2 Hercules as the world's toughest tow truck.

# M58 Wolf Smoke Generator Carrier

Thanks to the latest technology, the United States Army can strike at its enemies on the darkest nights and in the smoke and dust of the desert battlefield. But what if the army does not want others to see them? This is when the M58 Wolf comes to the rescue.

The M58 is not a weapon that harms the enemy, but it is just as valuable as any tank or gun. The Wolf is a Smoke Generator Carrier. In other words, it is a tanklike vehicle that makes thick clouds of white smoke. This smoke is meant to hide U.S. troops and vehicles from the enemy.

An M58 Smoke Generator Carrier is loaded onto a trailer to be moved to a different location.

The M58 Wolf usually operates in platoons, or groups, of seven. Its main job is to create smoke screens to hide ground troops and provide cover during rescue operations. When seven M58s are making smoke, they can hide an area more than half a mile (0.8 kilometer) wide by 3 miles (5 kilometers) long. The Wolf can produce a thick cloud of smoke for up to 90 minutes without refueling.

## How does the Wolf blow smoke?

Mounted on the back of the vehicle is a jet engine that burns diesel or jet fuel. When these liquid fuels are burned in the jet engine, they are turned into a vapor, which is a gas. It is like boiling water out of a pot. When this "fuel-gas" mixes with the cooler air, it condenses. That means that tiny droplets form as it changes back into a liquid. These droplets form what we call a fog.

A battlefield fills with smoke from an M58. This **tactic** helps U.S. troops escape and confuses the enemy.

# M931A1 Fox Reconnaissance System

The fox that you might see in the meadow is known for its sharp sense of smell. The United States Army also has a "fox" with its own very special and highly sensitive "sense of smell." It is called the Fox M931A1 **Reconnaissance** Vehicle. The Fox is one of the most important vehicles on the battlefield.

## Know It

The first gas ever used in combat was tear gas. It was used by the French against the Germans in 1914 during World War I. The first poison gas was used by the Germans in 1915. The substance was chlorine gas. Chlorine gas irritates the lungs and makes it very hard to breathe. Later in the war, the Germans used mustard gas which caused much more serious injuries.

The Fox could be described as a science laboratory on wheels. It collects samples from the air, water, and ground and then analyzes, or inspects, them with special instruments. Its crew is looking for signs of **contamination** on the battlefield from **weapons of mass destruction.**

The Fox M93A1 was a valuable tool in the Gulf War (1991). The probe at the front of the vehicle is testing the air for dangerous chemicals.

In World War I, soldiers counted on gas masks like these to protect them.

After World War I, the world powers decided that the use of poison gas was so horrible that it was banned from ever being used. Not all countries have obeyed that ban. In the late 1980s, Iraqi leader Saddam Hussein released chemical weapons on the Kurds, people living in northern Iraq who did not support his government.

These weapons can be nuclear, biological, or chemical. Unlike bombs and bullets, these weapons can hurt combat troops while remaining completely invisible. The Fox improves the chances for U.S. troops to control the battlefield and, more importantly, to survive.

## The Fox in action

The three-man crew inside the Fox begins its mission by checking special detectors and alarms that are built into the vehicle itself. One device, called the Remote Sensing Chemical Agent Alarm, is sensitive enough to detect dangerous chemical **agents** in the air from nearly 3 miles (5 kilometers) away. Once the danger is identified, the crew of the Fox sends the information to troop commanders. They can then stop or change the direction of the troops' movements on the battlefield. This can prevent the troops from being exposed to these invisible and very deadly weapons.

# HMMWV: You Can Just Call It Humvee

No matter what name they are known by, Humvees have become the best known light military trucks in the world. HMMWV stands for High-Mobility Multipurpose Wheeled Vehicle. It was designed as a replacement for the army's old and out-of-date jeep. It is several vehicles in one. It may be used as a command vehicle for officers overseeing the battlefield. The HMMWV can also carry troops, supplies, and equipment, and can serve as a combat ambulance. It can be used as a platform, or base, for a variety of weapons.

The HMMWV works well in all weather conditions and in the most difficult terrain. It has four-wheel drive, a powerful diesel engine, and high ground clearance. Because of its light weight and small size, the HMMWV can be easily transported to the battlefield by aircraft and even small helicopters. All models that carry weapons have armored

This heavily armored HMMWV and its crew keep watch.

bodies for added protection. There are specially equipped HMMWVs that can drive safely through water up to 5 feet (1 1/2 meters) deep.

Even if fully loaded with troops and equipment, the HMMWV can climb a 60-degree slope. (Straight up and down is 90 degrees.) A steep mountain road for passenger cars may be only about 15 degrees. The HMMWV can even travel safely on a side slope (tilted on its side) of up to 40 degrees. Most people cannot even stand up under those same conditions without falling.

High water does not slow down this Humvee.

By World War II, the U.S. Army was using jeeps like these. At the time, these jeeps were some of the newest vehicles.

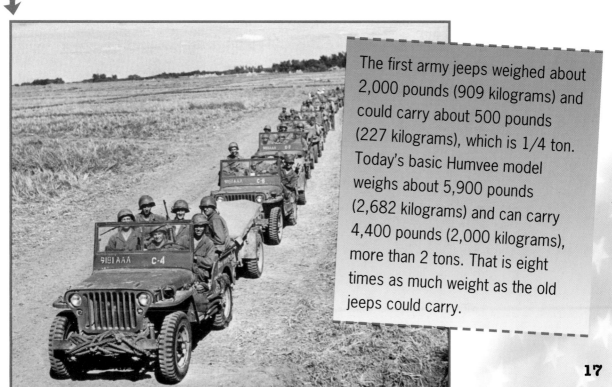

The first army jeeps weighed about 2,000 pounds (909 kilograms) and could carry about 500 pounds (227 kilograms), which is 1/4 ton. Today's basic Humvee model weighs about 5,900 pounds (2,682 kilograms) and can carry 4,400 pounds (2,000 kilograms), more than 2 tons. That is eight times as much weight as the old jeeps could carry.

# M109A6 Paladin Self-Propelled Howitzer

The Paladin is the army's latest and most advanced mobile (it can be moved around) cannon. Although it has tracks and a **turret** like a modern tank, there is one big difference. While the tank works best when fighting close to the enemy, the Paladin is designed to strike at targets that are miles away. It can be used at night and can fire in a 360-degree circle while still moving.

The word **howitzer** comes from the German word *haubitze*. It means catapult, which is a tool that throws objects.

## Paladin safety features

A long-range **howitzer,** or cannon, is important to an army. The problem in the past was that as soon as the cannon fired, it gave away its position and the enemy could fire on it. The Paladin can fire while moving. This makes it much harder for the enemy to find it. The Paladin can fire four rounds from its 155-millimeter (6-inch) gun and hit targets up to 18 miles (29 kilometers) away in less than 60 seconds.

The ability to fire while moving helps the Paladin's four-man crew avoid enemy fire. There is another form of protection built into every Paladin. The crew operates in a pressurized compartment that keeps them safe from the effects of nuclear, biological, and chemical attacks. This compartment is also equipped with secure voice and digital **communication** devices, which means the crew never has to leave during combat situations.

# The M109A6 Paladin Self-Propelled Howitzer

- Weight: 62,000 pounds or 31 tons

- Top speed: 35 miles (56 kilometers) per hour

- Crew: four, including the commander, gunner, loader, and driver

- Cruising range: 186 miles (299 kilometers), based on a fuel capacity of 133 gallons (503 liters). This is only 1.4 miles (2.25 kilometers) per gallon.

This M109A6 Paladin is shown using its firepower during the Gulf War (1991).

# OH-58D Kiowa Warrior: The U.S. Army's Spy in the Sky

The Kiowa Warrior is the army's newest flying spy. Officially, it is called an armed **reconnaissance** helicopter. Its main mission is to scout or inspect the battlefield for enemy troops and vehicles. The Kiowa Warrior can provide exact enemy locations to U.S. military aircraft and **personnel.** It can also be used for some rescue-and-recovery operations.

The Kiowa Warrior is also an attack aircraft. Attached to each side of the aircraft is a weapons system that can fire missiles. Each helicopter is also equipped with a machine gun.

## Know It

The Kiowa Warrior was developed from earlier versions of Kiowa helicopters. In the Persian Gulf in 1987, the military found they needed small, armed scout helicopters to keep an eye on enemy gunboats at night. The Kiowa Warrior was developed in less than 100 days.

An OH-58D Kiowa Warrior leaves a **communications** site in the desert during the Gulf War.

The mast-mounted sight has an advanced television camera to view targets far away. It also has a system that works by sensing temperature differences in the surroundings. This system allows the Kiowa Warrior to **navigate** and locate targets.

One of the key **surveillance** features of the Kiowa Warrior is the mast-mounted sight. It looks like a large periscope that you might see on a submarine. It is attached directly above the main rotor blades. This equipment allows the crew to see both during the day and at night. The crew can view the battlefield, identify targets, and report their exact locations at all times and under all conditions. The periscope design of the sight also helps protect the crew. The Kiowa Warrior can hide behind trees and other large objects with only the sight out in the open.

Two Kiowa Warrior helicopters can be transported in a C-130 aircraft. Parts of the tail, the main rotor blades, the mast-mounted sight, and the antenna can be removed.

# AH-64A/D Apache Attack Helicopters

The Apache is the United States Army's main attack helicopter. The Apache seeks out and destroys important targets and prevents enemy forces from moving on the battlefield. It is designed to operate during the day and at night, in all weather conditions. Apaches have the speed, firepower, and advanced technology to attack enemy forces that are on the ground and in the air.

This AH-64D Apache attack helicopter is traveling fully loaded with weapons.

The original version of the Apache is the AH-64A. For a while, it was considered the most advanced armed helicopter in the world. In the late 1990's a new version was built that is faster, "smarter," and far more powerful than the first. It is called the AH-64D Longbow.

The Apache helicopters have become one of the most useful fighting aircraft for the U.S. Army. During the Gulf War, Apaches destroyed more than 500 tanks and hundreds of other enemy vehicles.

## The Longbow

One amazing feature of the Longbow is its advanced targeting system. Using Fire Control Radar or FCR, the Longbow can locate and classify more than 128 targets and decide which are the 16 most dangerous. It can then send this information to other aircraft and begin an attack in less than 30 seconds. Using this same system, the Longbow can also hit a moving tank from a distance of more than 4 miles (6 kilometers), even if it is hidden by the dirt and smoke of the battlefield.

The AH-64D Longbow has some amazing weapons. One of them is the Hellfire missile. It has a fire-and-forget feature. This allows the Longbow's gunner to fire at several targets without having to control each missile until it hits its target. Along with the Hellfire missile, the Longbow also fires Hydra 70 rockets and has a 30 mm- (1.2 inch-) gun for air-to-air combat.

Each Apache has a crew of two: the pilot and the co-pilot/gunner. Apaches can fly at speeds above 140 miles (225 kilometers) per hour. The Army plans to change all of the AH-64As to AH-64Ds.

# AGM-114 Hellfire Missile

↑ This Apache AH-64 helicopter is armed with eight Hellfire missiles.

The name *Hellfire* comes from **HEL**icopter-Launched **FIRE**-and-forget missile. It is the main air-to-ground missile used by the Apache Longbow and many other combat helicopters. A missile is not a vehicle, but the Hellfire is part of what makes the Army's combat helicopters so powerful. Its main mission is to destroy tanks and other heavily **armored** vehicles.

In the first days of the Gulf War (1991), Hellfires were used to destroy Iraqi radar sites before the U.S. air attack. By the end of the war, the Hellfire had destroyed more than 500 Iraqi battle tanks.

The fire-and-forget technology of the Hellfire missile allows the Apache to release its sixteen Hellfire missiles at one time. Defending against one incoming Hellfire missile would be nearly impossible. Fighting all sixteen at one time would definitely be impossible.

The Hellfile missile is guided by a **laser.** After the missile is released, a laser beam is pointed at the target. This is done by either the Apache or by a vehicle on the ground. When the missile "sees" the laser, it simply follows the laser until it hits the target.

## Right on target

There is one common weakness in most enemy tanks and other armored vehicles. The heaviest armor is down low to protect against gunfire from other tanks. The tops of these vehicles normally have little armored protection. The top is the obvious place for the Hellfire to do the most damage. The Hellfire missile aims for the top of enemy vehicles. The straight-flying Hellfire can suddenly turn and go straight up just before it strikes its target. Then, just as suddenly, it dives straight down onto the tank's lightly armored top.

The Apache Longbow can fire the Hellfire missiles like it has fired these two rockets.

# LOSAT: Tank-Busting on a Budget

LOSAT stands for Line-Of-Sight Anti-Tank. It is an example of some of the U.S. Army's newest weapons technology. LOSAT is a lightweight, highly mobile (easily moved around) missile system. It is designed to seek out and destroy tanks and other **armored** vehicles.

Because of its small size, LOSAT can be easily moved to the battlefield by helicopters or cargo planes. This means the LOSAT can be set up and fired in almost every type of combat situation. It is attached to a special kind of Humvee and is operated by a crew of three. While LOSAT is not a fighting vehicle, without it, the Humvee would not be as useful.

A LOSAT fires a missile, right on target, even at night.

The LOSAT is loaded with four ready-to-fire missiles. It has up to eight additional missiles available on a towed trailer behind the Humvee.

When designing LOSAT, the army included the very latest missile technology. This new type of technology is called the **Kinetic** Energy Missile (KEM). The way it works is very simple. The end of each LOSAT missile has a long point called a penetrator rod. When the missile strikes its target at speeds approaching 1 mile (1.6 kilometers) per second, the rod blasts through even the heaviest armor, completely destroying the vehicle.

Enemy vehicles as far away as 2 miles (a little more than 3 kilometers) can be totally destroyed in a few blinks of the eye. The LOSAT's **laser** equipment lets them locate a target and fire the missile in only a few seconds. The LOSAT can also fire at more than one target at a time. If those targets are moving, the path of the missile can be changed as many times as needed until the targets are hit.

# M-220 TOW Antitank Missile

Another missile that helps make the Humvee vehicle so important is the TOW missile. TOW stands for **T**ube-Launched, **O**ptically tracked, **W**ire-guided missile. The latest version, called the TOW 2B, can go through armor that is more than 30 inches (75 centimeters) thick. Its small size and low cost have made TOW the most widely used antitank guided missile in the world. But even more important, the TOW missile has proven to be very accurate and successful.

How the TOW works is fairly simple and yet works very well. The gunner spots an enemy target through the sight. The gunner then fires the missile. Two very, very long spools of wire (their exact length is top secret) are

This soldier fires a TOW missile from his Humvee.

attached to the rear of the missile. As the missile heads toward its target, the two wires shoot out from the launcher. Signals to control direction are then sent through these wires to the missile's guidance system. The gunner keeps his sight on othe target. This makes sure that the missile will fly to where the gunner aimed it.

TOW missiles are usually mounted on a modified Humvee or Bradley Fighting Vehicle. Many U.S. military helicopters also carry the TOW system.

In one instance during the Gulf War, a TOW missile went completely through the Iraqi tank it was aimed at and then damaged another tank parked next to it.

This soldier is looking at the launch tube and sight of his TOW missile launcher.

# Patriot Air Defense System

These soldiers are servicing their truck-mounted Patriot Missile System.

The Patriot missile is one of the U.S. Army's most powerful defensive weapons. Its purpose is to protect U.S. combat troops from enemy missile attacks. The Patriot does this by intercepting, or catching, the attacking missile in midair before it can reach its target.

The Patriot missile is over 17 feet (5 meters) long and has 200 pounds (91 kilograms) of high explosives in its warhead. Within 20 feet (6 meters) of being launched, the Patriot missile is already traveling more than 700 miles (1,130 kilometers) per hour. It can strike at targets more than 50 miles (80 kilometers) away and can reach a top speed of over 3,000 miles (4,800 kilometers) per hour. The Patriot launch system can fire up to eight missiles and can be transported anywhere in the world in the giant C5A cargo plane. The launcher is mounted on a semitrailer that is towed by a 10-ton tractor.

The Patriot missile is very accurate because it has complicated guidance systems. One system uses **radar.** The radar beam works like a powerful flashlight as it sweeps the sky thousands of times every second, looking for enemy targets. Another system is called the Engagement Control Station or ECS. The ECS can completely control all parts of the Patriot system, from target identification to launching and tracking the missile.

The ECS is the only manned part of the Patriot system. It has a crew of three.

Already at supersonic speed, this Patriot missile is headed for its target.

# EFOGM Anti-Armor Missile

EFOGM stands for Enhanced **Fiber-Optic G**uided Missile. EFOGM is used mainly as an anti-tank missile, but it can also destroy enemy helicopters. It is easily transported by C-130 cargo aircraft and by the Chinook helicopter.

EFOGM is mounted on a HMMWV (Humvee). The launch vehicle that shoots the missile is known as the Fire Unit. It has a gunner and a driver. The command vehicle also has two people in it. The command vehicle has the computer that controls the flight of the EFOGM missile. Each launcher carries eight missiles that can be fired at a range of up to nine miles (14 kilometers).

The EFOGM system is easily transported by a CH-47 Chinook helicopter.

This HMMWV-mounted EFOGM launcher is ready to fire. When moving from one place to another, the launcher is lowered and lays flat on the Humvee.

## EFOGM in action

The EFOGM system uses technology known as **Non-Line-Of-Sight** (NLOS). This means that the operator does not need to see the target to hit it. This also means that the EFOGM crews can avoid being seen by the enemy while performing their mission. NLOS is like the technology used by the wire-guided TOW anti-tank missiles, but it has some important differences.

When an EFOGM is fired, fiber optic cables shoot out from the launcher. These are the types of cables that are used in many forms of everyday communication, including telephones and cable television. While in flight, EFOGM is able to take pictures of the ground below using an on-board video camera. It sends these pictures through the fiber optic cable back to the gunner. Using these pictures, the gunner decides which target the missile should go after. Instructions are then sent back through the cable to the missile, which then locks on to its target.

# Interim Armored Vehicles: Combat Transport of Tomorrow

In the future, the U.S. military may face more combat situations against small groups and governments similar to the situation in Afghanistan in the early 2000s. The army will have to react more quickly than ever before.

One way to do this is with the formation of **brigade** combat teams or BCTs. The goal of the teams is to be on the ground and ready to fight anywhere in the world within four days. The team's main transportation will be the Interim Armored Vehicle (IAV).

This Stryker Interim Armored Vehicle is on the move. The Stryker was named for two men who received the Medal of Honor. They had the same name but were not related.

The IAV may be easy to move on the battlefield, but first it has to get to the battlefield. The army often uses airplanes to transport its equipment.

The IAV moves fast and is highly mobile (easy to move around). It is light enough that it can be transported by the C-130 cargo plane anywhere in the world. It can carry ground troops at high speeds in even the most difficult battlefield conditions. It can also carry different kinds of weapon systems.

IAVs use wheels (like trucks) rather than tracks (like tanks). Wheels make the IAV run quieter and much faster than other kinds of **armored** vehicles. As an **infantry** carrier, a fully loaded IAV can travel on hard ground at speeds up to 60 miles (97 kilometers) per hour. The IAV can also be used to transport injured **personnel,** scout enemy positions, and pick up stranded troops.

When necessary, the IAV can also provde a lot of firepower. Its weapons include antitank guided missiles and machine guns.

# RAH-66 Comanche: Attack Helicopter for the 21st Century

This RAH-66 Comanche is on the first-ever flight test. It took place in 1996. It can take many years to develop new technologies for the armed services.

Some time in the early 2000s, the U.S. army has planned to introduce a new type of attack/**reconnaissance** helicopter. It is called the RAH-66 Comanche. Its main mission will be to locate and identify potential targets and to communicate this information to battlefield commanders. Comanche would then use its awesome firepower to destroy selected targets on the ground and in the air.

## The Comanche up close

The latest **stealth** technology has been used to make the Comanche very hard to track on **radar.** That means it will be safer to fly. It will also help the Comanche surprise the enemy. The body of the Comanche has been designed with different angles and shapes to confuse enemy radar systems. Also, the main rotor blades are made out a **composite** material instead of metal. This makes the Comanche much quieter. All this technology serves one main purpose: if enemy troops are not sure what they are looking at, they may not know what to do about it.

## The Comanche crew

The Comanche's two-person crew is made up of a pilot and copilot. Both people sit in a special **cockpit** that has been sealed to protect against biological and chemical warfare. The Comanche has special night vision systems, so the pilots can see in the dark.

The RAH-66 Comanche makes half as much noise as other helicopters. Its engines also create only one-fourth as much heat as other helicopters. This makes it very hard for the enemy to shoot it down with missiles that work by sensing the heat from their targets.

The pilots wear special helmets that display all important information directly in front of them on the helmet's visor. This means they never have to take their eyes off the sky while they are flying. Each cockpit also has a digital battlefield display. The display changes based on information from commanders on the ground.

# SmarTruck™: On the Road to the Future

It is not only soldiers who need to be kept safe in war zones. Sometimes government officials and advisers need to travel through dangerous areas. Soon, they may be riding in the army's SmarTruck™. No regular civilian truck has bullet-proof windows, an armored body, and can be equipped with a **laser**-guided missile system. It also has six wheels, not four.

If the enemy tries to follow the SmarTruck™, it can release a load of sharp tacks that will puncture the tires on the enemy's vehicle. Smoke can also be released, sort of like the M58 Smoke Generator Carrier, to confuse the enemy. The SmarTruck can also produce an oil slick and cause the enemy's vehicle to skid off the road.

SmarTruck™ II was displayed at the North America International Auto Show in January 2003, in Detroit. It has the same platform, or base, as a regular truck. But this truck can shoot laser-guided missiles.

Should someone approach the SmarTruck™, perhaps while it is stopped at a traffic light, the SmarTruck™ can shoot pepper spray 12 feet (3 1/2 meters). If enemy troops actually get to the door of the Smartruck, the electrified door handles will stun them.

Inside, the SmarTruck™ has a global positioning system and a computer. It registers the owner's fingerprints, and only the person with the "right" fingerprints can use the main controls in the truck. In the future, even the doors may require fingerprint identification.

The first SmarTruck™ was displayed in 2001. SmarTruck™ II was shown in January 2003. The new version can carry different sets of equipment depending on how it will be used. For example, if it is on a **humanitarian** mission, it can carry water purification equipment to provide safe water for the local people.

The SmarTruck™ is filled with the high-tech equipment. the "back seat" shown here is called the fighting compartment.

The SmarTruck's™ front seat is called the cockpit. The pilot (driver) can launch an unmanned air vehicle that sends video images to the truck's control center.

# ATACMS: High-Flying Missiles and Supersonic Bats

What if enemy **armored** forces could be destroyed without endangering U.S. pilots or ground forces? With the **A**rmy **Ta**ctical **M**issile **S**ystem (ATACMS), that possibility is now very real. One version, called Block II, uses "bats" to destroy tanks and other armored vehicles. The U.S. Army BAT is the **B**rilliant **A**nti-armor **T**echnology. This is a new kind of **submunition** that is designed to destroy armored vehicles from the sky.

A missile loaded with thirteen BATs is sent on a path that will take it directly above the enemy. When the missile is within range, it opens up and releases the BATs, which then glide down toward the ground.

BATs might be used with Unmanned Aerial Vehicles in the future.

**BAT** is released

**BAT** floats toward target

Target is hit

An ATACMS missile is fired. The BATs are inside the missile.

As the BATs glide downward, each one searches for an enemy target. It does this using several onboard sensors that detect sound and movement. Once the the BAT locks onto its target, it slowly floats down toward the target until it makes contact.

While all these BATs are doing their jobs, the soldiers who fired the missile are miles away and safe from harm. The ATCMS can operate 24 hours a day, in all kinds of weather. This means they are available to support ground troops whenever they need help.

# The Army's Unmanned Aircraft

The Tactical Unmanned Aerial Vehicle (TUAV) is one more example of how technology is changing how the U.S. Army fights battles. Its official name is the Shadow 200 TUAV. It is a pilotless aircraft designed to provide commanders on the ground with important information.

The Shadow TUAV performs **reconnaissance, surveillance,** and **target acquisition.** This means that the Shadow first locates the enemy. Then it keeps an eye on the enemy's movements. Finally, it provides the exact locations of enemy soldiers and equipment so the army knows where to aim and what to shoot at. The Shadow TUAV does all this with several complicated systems. They include a long-range camera, **laser** range-finder, **radar,** and a thermal, or heat, sensor.

Soldiers from an intelligence battalion prepare to launch a Shadow 200 Tactical Unmanned Aerial Vehicle.

The Shadow 200 TUAV in flight is loaded with technology but no pilot.

## A Shadow in flight

If you saw the Shadow 200 TUAV, you might think that it looks like a radio controlled model airplane. In a way, it is one. Its movements are programmed by a ground control station, or GCS. The GCS tells the Shadow 200 where to fly and what to look for, and then records the information it collects. The Shadow is capable of flying for more than five hours without refueling. It can fly as high as 15,000 feet (4,570 meters).

Amazingly, the engine for this high-flying aircraft produces only 38 horsepower. That's about the same as the outboard motor on a small fishing boat. It flies at a lazy 50 miles (81 kilometers) per hour. This is a perfect speed for taking high-altitude pictures of enemy troops and equipment on the ground. New versions will have longer wings, bigger engines, and be able to carry an even larger weapons.

# Arming the Vehicles of the Future: THEL

The Tactical High Energy Laser (THEL) may sound like science fiction, but it is very real. The use of **lasers** as weapons has been studied and researched for more than twenty years. With THEL, the army believes this technology is finally ready for today's battlefield.

Imagine the following situation: The enemy launches a surprise attack using weapons that suddenly appear out of nowhere, such as cruise missiles or short-range rockets. With almost no warning, the army would have to work hard to defend against such an attack. But what if the army had a weapon that could be fired at the speed of light, 186,000 miles (300,000 kilometers) per second? No matter how fast the attacking missiles were moving, they would be no match for a laser.

The THEL's beam director, shown here, aims the laser beam at the target.

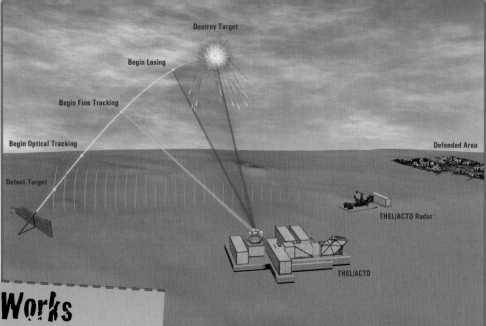

Destroy Target

Begin Lasing

Begin Fine Tracking

Begin Optical Tracking

Defended Area

Detect Target

THEL/ACTD Radar

THEL/ACTD

## How THEL Works

An enemy missile is detected by the fire-control **radar**. The radar figures out the flight path of the missile and "sends" that information to a tracking system. The tracking system includes the beam director, which aims the laser at the target. The laser causes the missile to heat up and then explode before it can hit a U.S. or other friendly target.

One of the greatest advantages to laser-based weapons systems is their mobility. Because they are rather small and lightweight, they can be mounted on a variety of platforms, or equipment. This

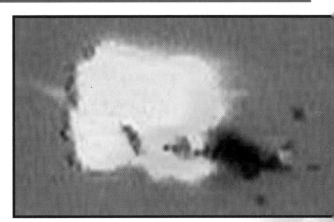

The THEL destroys an enemy missile before it can do any damage.

will make an ordinary vehicle into a fighting vehicle. Soon, this laser technology may become part of a space-based weapons system. If the United States was attacked with long-range missiles, such a system would be capable of detecting and destroying the missiles long before they reach their targets.

We might also see THELs mounted on the back of fast-moving combat vehicles or in a variety of aircraft. Laser technology has already provided the army with powerful laser-guided weapons. THEL is a new way to use this technology.

# Glossary

**agents** chemical substances which effect those who come in contact with them

**altitude** height

**armored** covered by metal

**artillery** large weapons, such as guns and missiles that require a crew to operate

**brigade** large unit of soldiers

**cockpit** place where the pilot or pilots of an aircraft sit

**comunications** sharing information

**composite** combination of materials used to make vehicles stronger and lighter

**contamination** battlefield is made unsafe or unhealthy by exposure to NBC weapons

**fiber-optic** method of sending commands and information through cables using light

**horsepower** measure of power that a horse produces when pulling something. Today, engines are compared to that standard. A small engine that is as powerful as 2 horses is labelled 2-horsepower

**humanitarian** something that helps people

**infantry** soldiers who fight on the ground

**kinetic** weapon that destroys its target by its impact rather than from an explosion

**laser** high-powered beam of light used in weapons and tracking systems

**line-of-sight** targeting something that can be seen by the weapon's operator

**navigate** find the right direction for travel

**personnel** the people employed in any work, business, or service

**pontoon** device which helps a vehicle float on water

**propulsion** force that pushes a craft or vehicle

**radar** system that used radio waves to find objects

**reconnaissance** seeking out information about locations and actions of the enemy

**stealth** aircraft design that uses unusual shapes and materials so that radar systems cannot find it

**submunition** small explosive device that is part of a larger weapon system

**surveillance** keeping an eye on the enemy without them knowing

**tactical** offensive weapons that are part of an army's battle plan

**tactic** plan

# More Books to Read

Gilbert, Adrian. *Going to War in World War I.* Danbury, Conn.: Franklin Watts, 2001.

Pitt, Matthew. *Apache Helicopter: The AH-64.* Danbury, Conn.: Children's Press, 2000.

An older person can help you read this book:

Stewart, Gail B. *Weapons of War: The Civil War.* San Diego, Calif.: Lucent Books, 2000.

# Places to Visit

U.S. Army Transportation Museum, 300 Washington Blvd, Besson Hall Fort Eustis, Virginia, 23604-5260, phone: (757) 878-1115
www.eustis.army.mil/dptmsec/museum.htm

U.S. Army Ordnance Museum, Aberdeen Proving Ground, Maryland, 21005, phone: (410) 272-3622
www.ordmusfound.org

# Index